ANXIETY

Strategies For Implementing Small Daily Habits To Effectively Cope With Anxiety And Overcome Pessimistic Thought Patterns

(An Essential Manual On Managing Anxiety And Mitigating The Effects Of Stress)

Ron Kramer

TABLE OF CONTENT

Comprehending The Influence Of The Ego In The Context Of Anxiety 1

Techniques For Implementing Progressive Muscle Relaxation 17

Nurturing Mindfulness: Liberating Yourself From Anxiety 29

Are You Experiencing Diminished Mental Capacity? 42

Genetics And Heredity 53

How To Be A Social Butterfly 68

Methods For Cultivating Detachment From One's Own Thoughts And Identity? 70

Assume Your Individual Responsibilities And Exercise Authority 82

Rapid Strategies To Employ When Experiencing Elevated Levels Of Stress 86

Reading The Eyes 94

Anxiousness As A Response To Ambiguity 105

Comprehending The Influence Of The Ego In The Context Of Anxiety

If the objective is to reconfigure neural pathways to effectively address anxiety, it is imperative to tackle the prominent issue at hand. We are discussing the concept of ego, which is inherent in most individuals, even those who attempt to feign its absence. The ego refers to the internalized voice within oneself. It is crucial for the inner self to strive for superiority in relation to its peers. If one fails to appropriately restrain their ego, they may succumb to a state of illusion. When an individual lacks the ability to regulate their ego, the ego assumes control. When such an occurrence takes place, one of its primary objectives is to identify circumstances that do not pose a risk to its well-being. The ego is driven by a desire for security. It endeavors to consolidate its position and attain a sense of gratification. One may conceptualize their ego as a dependent child that incessantly craves indulgence. In this scenario, the psychological content in question would manifest itself as a source of continuous reassurance, praise, and approval. The origin lies in your consistent access to a secure refuge, as the ego is averse to the potential vulnerability of being uncovered. If I were to hold the conviction that I possess extraordinary talent or status, despite lacking tangible accomplishments or financial resources to substantiate such claims, I would actively seek individuals who are inclined to validate and reinforce this self-deception. Any individual or entity that lacks alignment with the ego will invariably engender a state of distress known as anxiety. The underlying cause for this phenomenon stems from the fact that when a circumstance, individual, location, or object fails to support the delusion that the ego has constructed, it consequently instills a sense of apprehension. This is among the factors contributing to the challenges typically faced by individuals with anxiety when it comes to immersing themselves in unfamiliar or unfamiliar environments. It constitutes a significant factor contributing to the failure of numerous individuals to transcend their socio-economic origins. Once more, uncertainty and apprehension serve as a formidable combination instigating fear. However, when compounded with the self-centered aspect, it can manifest into an exceedingly tormenting experience. When an individual's ego is harmed, they will endeavor to obtain reassurance in the most suitable manner they are familiar with. For certain individuals, this could manifest as indulgence in comforting edibles, while for others, it might manifest as recourse to substances such as drugs or alcohol, engaging in promiscuous activities, or aimlessly indulging in entertainment, among other avenues. An individual who experiences apprehension when being in the company of others could potentially be characterized as being timid or exhibiting antisocial behavior. Does this individual harbor concerns about being disliked by others? Do they have concerns that their limitations may come into focus, particularly when the individuals observing them are of exceptional caliber? Does this individual possess a fear that revealing their true self would result in rejection? The ego, as it were, resists such vulnerability since most individuals perceive themselves as the primary focus, the central figure, the main event, and the distinguished guest. Anxiety may arise whenever any of these aspects come under threat. Hence, the inquiry arises as to how one should tackle this matter. What strategies can be employed to transcend the ego? The most effective approach would be for you to adopt a self-critical mindset. Should you possess awareness of a particular weakness, it becomes imperative for you to diligently address and rectify said weakness, or alternatively, identify and further enhance a strength to such an extent that it surpasses the impact of the weakness. You do honest self-assessments. As an illustration, in the event that experiencing difficulty in captivating the attention of individuals from the opposite gender, one must inquire as to the aspects of their own persona that may be accountable for this predicament. Perhaps you may need to refine your conversational abilities or work on projecting a more approachable demeanor. The underlying message is that it is imperative to maintain humility and engage in sincere self-evaluation in order to deconstruct oneself and prioritize personal growth. You will discover that this approach significantly diminishes the influence of anxiety upon you.

What Is Capacity?
Capacity refers to an individual's inherent capability and aptitude to perform a task with proficiency. It could alternatively be characterized as the aptitude, proficiency, and expertise that one employs in the pursuit of a specific objective. Your capabilities have a tendency to flourish as you mature and acquire knowledge. As an illustration, a

young individual may experience repeated instances of imbalance and subsequent falls prior to acquiring the skill of walking. Your potential can be constrained by your degree of personal growth and the extent of expertise or understanding you have accumulated. While it is possible for anyone to aspire to pursue a career in medicine, it is only through the completion of a rigorous medical education and specialized training that individuals can attain the esteemed title of a doctor. To a certain extent, contingent upon one's level of expertise and understanding, one possesses the capability (capacity) to execute specific assignments, while being incapable of undertaking others. Enhancing one's capacity becomes feasible solely through the accumulation of experience and knowledge.

Your capacity refers to your ability to accept and handle tasks and responsibilities. It varies among each individual. Certain individuals possess a predisposition for meticulousness. Others may possess a propensity for holistic thinking and strategic analysis. Certain individuals demonstrate unwavering dedication, agility, dynamism, and a wealth of expertise, among other noteworthy qualities. Additional individuals possess adaptability, considerate nature, composure, ingenuity, and more. Our capacity encompasses both inherent inclinations and abilities that can be cultivated. Certain tasks come naturally to us. While we can provide training for others to develop their skills.

Capacity encompasses a wide spectrum of aptitudes, encompassing not only the intangible qualities of patience, kindness, leadership, organization, creativity, thoughtfulness, candor, diligence, communication, etc., but also the concrete competencies such as writing, presenting, culinary expertise, computer design, and numerous others.

Capacity is intricately connected to one's aptitude. Consider capacity as the receptacle and ability as the substance that occupies it. As the capacity increases, the potential for the infusion of ability also expands.

Presented herewith are several widely recognized categories of abilities:

Domain expertise: Specialized knowledge relating to a particular subject, industry, profession, or cultural context.

Tacit knowledge, or expertise acquired through extensive practice or hands-on experience, such as engaging in football or engaging in entrepreneurship.

Learning: The aptitude to assimilate and retain novel knowledge and implement it in one's daily existence.

Research entails the systematic exploration and evaluation of diverse sources of knowledge, leading to the discovery of novel information.

Problem resolution: Analyzing problems in order to ascertain the underlying cause and devise suitable remedies.

Emotional intelligence refers to the aptitude of comprehending and interpreting the emotions of others, enabling individuals to effectively navigate diverse social contexts and adapt their communication style accordingly.

Creativity: Engaging in the process of ideation to generate innovative concepts that defy traditional notions and uncover alternative approaches for problem solving or task execution.

Approach: Devising strategic measures to address precise challenges or attain predetermined objectives.

Talent vs. Skill

It is a prevalent phenomenon for individuals to exhibit confusion between talents and skills, and conversely, despite their distinct descriptions denoting contrasting abilities. Talents, such as natural aptitudes, are innate capabilities conferred at birth, while skills are acquired proficiencies cultivated over time and through experience. Talents can be cultivated and enhanced through conscientious effort and suitable mentorship, whereas skills can solely be acquired through unwavering perseverance and diligent application.

An individual endowed with the natural aptitude for oratory can captivate any audience effortlessly, without needing significant prior groundwork. They possess inherent sociability and can cultivate emotional intelligence through deliberate efforts, which amplifies their innate aptitude for public speaking. This is distinct from an individual who is required to attend educational institutions for the purpose of acquiring skills in public speaking and exert substantial efforts towards cultivating an amiable demeanor. Ultimately, their proficiency in delivering speeches in public is a product of acquired expertise, rather than an inherent gift.

Every person possesses a unique combination of innate talents and acquired skills. It is not possible to assert that utilizing talents is superior to utilizing skills, or that possessing expertise in a subject is preferable to having an innate aptitude for it. The worth of abilities and aptitudes is contingent upon the manner in which each individual harnesses their innate attributes, paired with the knowledge acquired to embrace their Ikigai.

While it may be straightforward to ascertain your aptitudes through tangible evidence, discerning your inherent talents can present a challenge. One might mistakenly consider their talents as an inherent character attribute, such as being adept at conversation. There is also a possibility that you might be inclined to dismiss your inherent abilities, particularly if you were raised in an environment where your distinct talents were regarded as unfavorable. Below are three methods you can employ to ascertain your inherent abilities, enabling you to leverage them while pursuing your Ikigai:

Reflection

It is often more convenient for many individuals to discern the talents exhibited by others rather than acknowledging their own abilities. It is a universally recognized truth that we tend to be highly self-critical when evaluating our own strengths.

Nevertheless, it is crucial for you to grasp the fact that, like any other individual, you possess inherent talents and aptitudes. There does not exist a subset of the human population characterized by exceptional or paranormal capabilities that freely traverse the earth. Every individual, irrespective of their origin or unique characteristics, is inherently endowed with talents.

Upon acknowledging this reality about oneself, one will encounter reduced opposition when contemplating the innate talents that manifest effortlessly. There is no need for exhaustive contemplation since these capabilities manifest effortlessly regardless. You simply need to reflect on prior instances when you demonstrated exceptional proficiency with minimal time or effort, or when others sought your guidance in relation to that specific skill.

One may also contemplate upon the endeavors in which they excelled during their adolescent years. Alternatively, one could convey the same sentiment in a more formal tone as follows: "Or the various forms of commendation or favorable remarks that you have received throughout your lifetime from different individuals." One can also engage in introspection regarding their most exceptional abilities, thereby discerning recurring patterns or themes indicative of specific talents. As an illustration, individuals with a notably imaginative mind and proficient storytelling skills may possess an inherent aptitude for pursuits such as writing, poetry, or the creation of films.

Articulate your abilities through a collaborative ideation session wherein you record your thoughts on a sheet of paper. Please write to the fullest extent possible. It may be helpful to set a timer and brainstorm for a fixed amount of time, say 5 minutes. Please expeditiously and comprehensively articulate these ideas. And abstain from the evaluation or judgment of your ideas. Not yet. We will undertake this task to a certain extent in the subsequent phase, known as Assessment.

Assessment

You have now been presented with a multitude of ideas pertaining to potentially beneficial talents. It is imperative to conduct a thorough examination of them. Please carefully examine each item on your list. Dig in. Delve deep into the essence of your skills. Are there fundamental abilities that serve as the foundation for what is already presented on the document? Are there any skills or abilities possessed by their sister that are, in any manner, correlated or otherwise linked? Would you be able to provide a broader scope and identify larger or more overarching concepts?

Please evaluate your proficiency level in each of these skills. Utilize any system that suits your needs. The rating system has a range of 1 to 5 stars, depicting a spectrum from contentment to utmost satisfaction. Alternatively, it can also employ a scale from novice to exceptional, allowing for a broader and more nuanced evaluation. Just be realistic. Be honest. Do not overestimate or underestimate your capabilities.

Furthermore, undergoing a standardized evaluation will provide you with the affirmation you seek. There exist numerous online talent assessments that are cost-free and yield reliable outcomes. I would like to suggest the Myers-Briggs Type Indicator (MBTI) and the Clifton Strengths test as two viable options. The MBTI assessment is available at no cost and can facilitate an understanding of one's personality type, providing valuable insights into innate abilities and areas of proficiency. The Clifton Strengths test is a fee-based web-based evaluation that assists individuals in identifying their unique talents by utilizing a series of 177 paired statements. While these assessments can be of considerable utility, it is important to bear in mind that they serve as mere instruments intended to assist in comprehending various facets of one's identity. They can point you in the direction toward finding your talents and confirm strong inclinations that you already have.

Grounding

By this juncture, it is expected that you have a document at your disposal containing a comprehensive record of potential talents as well as the outcomes derived from your completed assessments pertaining to your talents and personality type. Now, you may appraise the amassed data and identify recurrent concepts or patterns indicative of your inherent talents. To rephrase that in a formal tone: "To elaborate, considering the feedback or experiences you have acquired throughout your upbringing, as well as the outcomes of your assessments, what areas would you assertively identify as your areas of talent?" Once you have ascertained your inherent abilities, you may proceed to conduct meticulous inquiry pertaining to each talent, thereby delving into the diverse array of applications or potential for augmentation they possess.

Techniques For Implementing Progressive Muscle Relaxation

Locate a suitable environment characterized by minimal noise and a lack of disturbances. If one finds oneself prone to distraction while at home, it might be advisable to opt for a public environment. Please ensure that you communicate your preference to not be interrupted or disturbed for a specified duration. Please set your cellular phone to silent mode, or preferably, refrain from bringing it along.

- Assume a prone position on the floor or recline in a chair.

Please ensure to loosen any constricting garments, and kindly remove spectacles or disengage contact lenses.

- Maintain the positioning of your hands either on your lap or delicately placed on the arms of the chair. Providing support to your arms will facilitate their complete relaxation, all the while preventing them from hanging loosely.
- Inhale and exhale deliberately, ensuring a slow and steady rhythm. Practice your diaphragmatic breathing. Inhale through

your nasal passage, followed by an exhalation through your oral cavity, maintaining a steady and synchronized pattern.

- Direct your complete concentration towards your forehead, exerting pressure on the muscles located in that area for a duration of approximately 15 seconds. Ensure that the remainder of your body is in a state of relaxation, with exclusive focus on tensing solely the muscles of the forehead.
- Experience the sensation of muscles contracting and becoming tense. Please endeavour to concentrate solely on this sensation.

Please proceed to count in a deliberate manner for a duration of 30 seconds, after which you can gradually release the built-up tension. Experience the contrast between the tension in your muscles and the state of relaxation they may assume. Persist until full relaxation is achieved in your forehead.

- Subsequently, direct your attention to your jaw, deliberately contracting and

maintaining tension in the muscles for a period of 15 seconds.
- Gradually relax the muscles over the course of thirty seconds.

Next in line are the neck and shoulders. Elevate your shoulders towards your ears, intensifying the strain and maintaining the position for a duration of 15 seconds. Allow a duration of 30 seconds for the release.

Kindly proceed by gradually curling your hands into a closed grip and gently retracting them towards your torso. Hold for 15 seconds. Relieve the tension and proceed to count for a duration of 30 seconds.

- Engage the muscles of the buttocks, incrementally increasing tension for a duration of 15 seconds, followed by a gradual release of the muscle tension over a period of 30 seconds.
- Gradually elevate the tension in your lower limbs, with a particular focus on the calf muscles and quadriceps. Exert maximum pressure and subsequently release gradually within a span of 30 seconds.

Finally, with regards to the feet. Gradually intensify the pressure exerted on your feet and toes while diligently contracting and fully engaging the associated muscles. Gradually and methodically let go over a span of 30 seconds, and take note of the relaxation taking hold.

While engaging in this practice, it is advantageous to focus your attention on individual body parts sequentially. Observe with fascination the gradual dissipation of all accumulated tension within, akin to the gradual melting of butter when placed under the sun's gentle warmth. Indulge in the sensation of profound relaxation that envelops your entire being, while maintaining a deliberate rhythm of slow, deep, and even breaths. Evidently, it is imperative to abstain from tensing muscles that have already been relaxed. When one rises, it is advised to primarily engage and tense the muscles in the feet, while keeping the rest of the body in a state of relaxation. Otherwise, it would be necessary to initiate the process anew.

Autogenic Training

Autogenic training can be likened to the practice of meditation. In the context of autogenic training, individuals engage in the repetition of affirmations pertaining to specific bodily regions, with the purpose of exerting an influence on the functioning of their autonomic nervous system. This encompasses the measurement of your cardiac rhythm. Fundamentally, it pertains to the concept of visualizing. If one employs the power of visualization to manifest their desired reality, it shall materialize as reality.

Autogenic training was initially presented in 1932 as a method of inducing relaxation by renowned German psychiatrist Johannes Heinrich Schultz. He observed that individuals subjected to hypnosis entered a state of tranquility, wherein they encountered profound sensations of warmth. He aimed to replicate that experience by implementing strategies that minimized feelings of anxiety and tension. It is believed that through the repetition of statements pertaining to the sensations of warmth and heaviness in specific body areas, a beneficial impact on the autonomic nervous system is purported. While autogenic training may not be as widely recognized for its relaxation benefits compared to other methods, a study conducted in 2008 demonstrated its efficacy in treating anxiety. When considering individuals suffering from social anxiety disorder, autogenic training has proven effective in inducing relaxation and alleviating symptoms when utilized as a supplementary therapeutic approach, particularly in its role of promoting a sense of relaxation and composure within social and performance-oriented contexts. With regular practice, uttering the phrase "I am calm" has the potential to induce a state of relaxation at the moment it is spoken.

Furthermore, in the event that you are afflicted by any psychiatric or medical ailments, it is strongly recommended that you seek counsel from a healthcare professional prior to commencing this or any alternative relaxation method. Autogenic training is contraindicated for individuals with severe emotional or mental disorders. In the event that you commence this activity, it is imperative that you promptly discontinue if you encounter intense anxiety, agitation, or any other adverse effects during or following the training session.

Methods for Engaging in Autogenic Training

Similar to the aforementioned relaxation technique and meditation, it is imperative to seek out an environment devoid of disturbances and characterized by tranquility. Assume a comfortable posture and take off eyewear, such as glasses or contact lenses. Please ensure that any tight-fitting garments are either loosened or removed, and kindly place your hands either on the armrests of the chair or in your lap. Please practice calm, deliberate breaths, ensuring they are slow, deep, and synchronized with even intervals, drawing air from the abdominal region.

Engage in the act of quietly articulating the subsequent statements:

● Verbally affirm to oneself, "I am in a state of complete tranquility."

● Direct your attention to your arms and internally affirm, "I perceive a profound sensation of weight in my upper limbs." Repeat this statement precisely six times.

- Subsequently, express serenity by stating "I am composed and tranquil."
- Direct your attention to your arms once more and articulate, "I perceive a notable warmth in my arms." Recite this phrase a total of 6 times.
- Subsequently, proceed by asserting, "I am in a state of complete composure."
- Direct your attention to your lower limbs and state, "The weightiness of my legs is quite pronounced." Say this 6 times.
- Proceed by stating, "I am in a state of complete tranquility"

Direct your attention to your lower limbs once more and articulate, 'I am experiencing a considerable warmth in my legs'. Say this 6 times.

- Subsequently, state, "I am entirely composed."
- Repeat to yourself the affirmation: 'My cardiac rhythm remains tranquil and consistent.' Say this 6 times
- Subsequently, assert "I am in a state of complete tranquility."

- State to oneself, "I am experiencing a state of tranquil and uniform respiration." Say this 6 times
- Proceed with stating, "I am entirely composed."
- Repeat to oneself, "My abdominal region is experiencing a sensation of warmth." Utter this affirmation six times.

Proceed by stating, "I am in a state of complete tranquility."

- Repeat the mantra, "My forehead is pleasantly cool," six times.
- Subsequently, proceed by stating, "I am perfectly composed."
- Appreciate the sensations of relaxation, encompassing the feelings of warmth and a soothing sense of heaviness. Take delight in it and wholeheartedly accept it.
- Once you feel prepared, silently affirm to yourself, "Maintain a stable arm position, take deep breaths, and open your eyes."

Guided Imagery

On numerous occasions, have you ever desired to embark on a departure, relinquishing all obligations and embarking towards a sun-kissed tropical destination or secluding oneself within a rustic log retreat nestled amidst a snow-laden hillside? A scarcity of individuals possess both the necessary time and financial means to actualize their profound desires. However, a viable alternative presents itself in the form of guided imagery. This method entails leveraging all sensory faculties to imagine oneself immersed in a state of utter relaxation within a chosen environment. Once your mental state aligns, your physical being will naturally follow suit, transitioning into a state of complete relaxation.

The practice of guided imagery gained recognition only in the post-1980s era coinciding with the advancement of psychoneuroimmunology, a field of research that investigates the interplay between psychology, neurology, and immunology. This research has demonstrated that the cognitive and emotional states of individuals exert an impact on the physiological processes of the human body. The objective of utilizing guided imagery is to engage in the cognitive and emotional processes of generating positive thoughts and emotions by envisioning positive scenarios. This in turn facilitates advantageous effects on one's physical well-being.

The utilization of guided imagery as a means of inducing relaxation proves to be a beneficial methodology for individuals who suffer from social anxiety disorders. One frequently envisions or conjures the sounds of the ocean lapping against a sun-drenched Tropical Island, or reclining in front of a grand, crackling hearth as the snow gently descends outdoors. The concept is to conceive of a setting that induces relaxation, rather than adhering to prescribed imagery. The specific setting holds minimal significance; what holds utmost importance is immersing oneself in the full sensory experience - every sound, every scent, and every visual - effectively transporting oneself to that location when one's eyes are shut.

It is imperative to consult a medical professional prior to attempting this, especially if you have a pre-existing medical condition. Please take note that engaging in guided imagery exercises may induce drowsiness. It is advisable to avoid practicing them when time constraints are present. Optimal timing is typically before or during bedtime in the evening.

Nurturing Mindfulness: Liberating Yourself From Anxiety

Mindfulness is a cognitive exercise that entails redirecting attention away from thoughts and emphasizing present moment awareness. Cognitive experiences encompass an individual's intellectual processes, encompassing the realms of thoughts, recollections, and emotions that reside within their conscious mind at any given moment. These experiences encompass reflections upon the past, concerns regarding the future, and other subliminal cognitive processes.

A significant portion of our stress and anxiety originates from our preoccupations with the future or the emotional responses evoked by our past encounters. Your apprehension is heightened by concerns pertaining to the probable outcomes in the forthcoming times. If you have a tendency to become entrapped by past events, it is probable that a significant portion of your time will be devoted to experiencing emotional distress. When we are pressed for time, we rely on our cognitive recollections rather than our immediate circumstances to inform our decision-making.

Consequently, mindfulness emerges as a highly efficacious approach for managing stress. It diverts your attention away from adverse thoughts and emotions, enabling you to concentrate and fully savor the present experience. When it pertains to surmounting anxiety, mindfulness emerges as one of the most efficacious techniques.

Mindfulness is usually practiced by following the most principles of achieving a balanced spirit and inner peace. These include:

Displaying complete awareness of oneself, others, and the environment.

Deliberate attention and mindful observation of one's surroundings.

Conveying circumstances and personal encounters through verbal expression.

iv. Opting not to focus on the thoughts

and emotions pertaining to previous or forthcoming occurrences.

Maintaining a neutral stance towards cognitive encounters.

Efficient strategies for managing anxiety involve the utilization of basic mindfulness techniques such as:

Breathing techniques

One can attain a state of inner tranquility and relieve psychological stress by engaging in rhythmic respiration techniques. Engaging in deep, focused respiration exclusively dedicated to regulating one's breath can yield remarkable results in alleviating feelings of anxiety.

The advantage of this approach is its ability to be executed in any location and at any given moment. Irrespective of whether you are engaged in your daily responsibilities or ensnared by vehicular congestion, the practice of mindful breathing techniques can be undertaken at any given moment.

The key is to direct your complete concentration towards the rhythmic respiration that occurs when deeply inhaling and then exhaling at a slow pace. While engaging in this action, one will perceive a gradual alleviation of pressure, as a sense of tranquility gradually predominates.

If you are able to locate a tranquil setting in which to engage in your deep breathing exercises, it would be advantageous as it would minimize interruptions. You will assume a seated, standing, or reclined position as you engage in the practice of this mindfulness technique.

Position your right arm beneath your diaphragm, situated precisely above your navel. As you inhale deeply, proceed to steadily count to six, directing your complete concentration towards the ascent of your chest. Take a gradual, deliberate breath out and once more, disregard all distractions except for the sensation of your chest lowering with each exhalation.

You are welcome to engage in the repetition of this system as frequently as you desire within the course of a day or whenever you perceive the onset of anxiety.

Meditation

The practice of meditation involves the deliberate regulation of breathing, the intentional release of muscle tension, and the utilization of imagination in order to attain a state of mindfulness and emotional equilibrium. Meditation can prove to be a highly efficacious methodology for cultivating mindfulness, as it enhances introspection and mitigates the distress triggered by cognitive phenomena.

In addition, the practice of meditation enhances cognitive acuity and facilitates the effective regulation of one's emotional state. This grants you enhanced command over your actions and conduct. Whether you are a novice or well-versed in the practice of meditation, establishing a regular pattern that suits your needs is of utmost importance.

An ideal meditation regimen is one that can be seamlessly incorporated into your daily routine. There is no necessity for you to enroll in a meditation class in order to derive benefits from the practice of mindful meditation. A multitude of virtual resources, including applications, are available that offer guided meditation.

c) Yoga

Yoga can be regarded as a form of physical activity that fosters a state of emotional and mental equilibrium. It integrates physical, mental, and spiritual practices to attain inner tranquility. Yoga serves as an exceptionally efficacious mindfulness practice to address anxiety. In addition, it is beneficial for one's physical well-being and aids in maintaining a fit physique.

The practice of yoga enhances one's self-awareness and affords improved management of adverse emotions such as anxiety, jealousy, and anger. Additionally, it fosters cognitive lucidity, thereby allowing for improved decision-making for both personal and relational matters.

The inherent advantage of practicing yoga lies in its characteristic of being a low-impact physical activity, rendering it universally safe and suitable for individuals of any age or body mass. Numerous yoga classes catered to beginners can be found online and at various fitness centers. By engaging the services of a certified yoga instructor, you can readily access the multitude of benefits that practicing yoga offers in effectively managing your anxiety.

Eleventh day: Ensure Sufficient Rest
Insufficient sleep will not alleviate your anxiety. Indeed, this will simply exacerbate your stress levels and result in a negative emotional state. Inadequate sleep additionally impairs cognitive function, compromising one's ability to formulate rational judgments or decisions. All tasks will present themselves as formidable, consequently intensifying your state of anxiety. In the absence of mental concentration, trivial matters appear magnified beyond their actual significance. You might fail to

perceive straightforward solutions due to fatigue impeding your ability to grasp them. Your capacity to make sound judgments is compromised, not due to ineptitude, but rather as a result of impaired logical reasoning caused by sleep deprivation.

May I inquire as to your abilities and skills?

One can commence by establishing a nocturnal sleep regimen. Initially, consider the tasks that necessitate completion upon waking up and proceed to transcribe them into a written enumeration. This will prompt your mind to acknowledge that you have formulated a strategy to tackle the following day, thus granting permission to fully disconnect for the night. Afterwards, make preparations for the upcoming day. For instance, if you are contemplating a visit to your workplace, ensure to promptly prepare your professional attire, midday meal, and automobile keys. Therefore, you will experience restful sleep with a sense of preparedness for the forthcoming day, eradicating any need for apprehension.

After you have carefully devised your schedule for the following day, proceed to identify the specific activities you wish to incorporate into your nocturnal routine. You may opt for some calming music to facilitate relaxation as you get ready to retire for the night. One may choose to indulge in a serene bath to alleviate the burdens of the day, simultaneously embracing the solace of an engaging literary piece. Regardless of the activities you decide on, make sure to schedule them consistently at a fixed time every evening. In this manner, as you commence engaging in these activities, your mind will initiate the process of preparing for sleep. Adhere to your established nocturnal regimen and permit it to facilitate sleep enhancement while decreasing levels of stress and anxiety.

Do Fun Activities

Engaging in enjoyable activities is unparalleled in terms of its capacity to uplift one's spirits. In the forthcoming days, our attention will be directed towards engaging activities that can be undertaken to effectively cope with anxiety.

Day 12: Socialize

It is alluring to isolate oneself and avoid social interactions when experiencing feelings of depression or anxiety. Regrettably, this is of no benefit to you. The greater your propensity for avoidance towards others, the more you fuel your anxiety. It should be noted that one should not abruptly adopt a lifestyle of excessive revelry. One can discover a harmonious equilibrium, enabling them to partake in interactions with others and forge significant connections. Bear in mind that there is no expectation for you to epitomize perfection. One can only become at ease in the presence of others by exerting oneself.

You may commence by contacting or messaging your relatives. Allocate a specific day in your weekly schedule devoted to initiating communication with your relatives or friends. Engage in conversation with them to ascertain the current circumstances of their lives. As one develops a strong commitment to fostering positive interpersonal connections, it becomes apparent that certain matters transcend across all individuals. They exert influence on not only your own self, but also on others around you. As you gain insight into the aspirations, apprehensions, and concerns of individuals, you will acquire the ability to place your own anxieties and concerns into a broader context. Rather than permitting anxiety to overpower you, you will acquire the ability to identify proactive approaches to resolve issues.

Day 13: Engage in a Stroll

Engaging in physical exercise is highly effective in diminishing one's levels of anxiety. This phenomenon occurs as a result of the body's production of endorphins during exercise or any form of physical activity. Endorphins function as innate analgesics, aiding in the recuperation of both mind and body. When one partakes in physical activity, they can alleviate stress, regulate mood, diminish tension, and enhance their self-esteem. Taking a leisurely stroll is among the various strategies you can employ to augment your physical activity levels.

While in motion, direct your focus towards the action of your footsteps, rather than allowing your thoughts to wander to other matters. This practice can be classified as a form of meditation. Directing your attention towards the manner in which your feet make contact with the surface will help to maintain immediate mental awareness. Therefore, upon concluding your stroll, your thoughts will be calmed and your understanding will be enhanced. Initially, you may commence with a 10-minute stroll and subsequently advance the duration, should you be able to do so. It is crucial to allocate a few minutes daily for the purpose of engaging in a walk. Engaging in a practice of walking meditation affords your brain a respite and curbs the escalation of anxiety.

Are You Experiencing Diminished Mental Capacity?

Do you believe that you are experiencing a decline in your mental faculties? Do you perceive a sense of unreality in your surroundings? Is it fair to say that your perception of reality may be somewhat distorted? Do you perceive any sense of experiencing heightened emotional or cognitive instability? As it is commonly said, the direction of one's thoughts determines the course of one's actions. We can only hope that this is not the case.

I am present with the intention of providing you with as much assistance as I possibly can. As previously stated, I am in no way a medical professional. I do not make any attempts to exude such behavior. You are gaining first-hand insights and perspectives from an actual individual. In addition to my own experiences, I have received testimonials from various individuals who consistently relay similar narratives. I am experiencing a severe mental distress.

You are not, as I would like to reiterate. You are not experiencing a loss of mental faculties. It is indeed necessary for you to acquire the skills to regulate your thoughts. That particular aspect of anxiety can be considered the most challenging. Exercising cognitive control, effectively managing negative and irrational thoughts. Rest assured, if you allow them, they will readily exploit your trust and bring about detrimental consequences to your existence.

Herein lies my perspective on perceiving a potential state of mental disarray. I have acquired and continue to acquire the necessary skills to maintain a grounded perception of reality.

It commenced with the onset of my initial episode of acute anxiety. As I traversed my abode, an abrupt onset of severe tunnel vision befell me. It appeared as though the ground was in motion. I had to take a seat and engage in prayer, hoping that it was not the case. I remained seated in that location temporarily. Attempting to reassure myself that there are no inherent flaws within me. Indeed, engaging in self-conversation is acceptable; however, refrain from responding to yourself. lol. I assumed a poised posture and regained mental clarity, at least temporarily. I refer to this particular moment, as it began to occur frequently over a span of approximately six months. I must admit that upon embarking on this anxiety-inducing journey. Various events and occurrences impact both your mental and physical well-being. If one has experienced these peculiar instances of a distorted reality, it becomes apparent what I am alluding to. They can evoke a great deal of fear. This is the point where one begins to believe they are experiencing a loss of sanity. I neglected to make the previous point that immediately subsequent to that event, the floor began to shift. I experienced a distressing episode of intense anxiety. In my estimation, the attack endured for approximately five minutes. I am aware that you may hold the perception that the duration is not lengthy. Nevertheless, if one has experienced a panic attack, they are well aware of the considerable duration it entails. Typically, the duration of an assault is relatively short.

Allow me to propose an additional unconventional and eccentric idea. I believe this is something with which you can connect. I gradually developed a persistent sensation, occurring on a daily basis without exception. Given that I was conversing continuously, I had the impression that my vitality was gradually waning, almost to the point of expiration. Indeed, simply recline and meet one's demise. In my estimation, this chronic anxiety and recurrent instances of panic far exceed the severity of symptoms experienced during menopause. I am curious if any women who have experienced menopause can empathize? If one is a male individual, it is understood that the path one traverses can be arduous. Indeed, the perturbation lies within the confines of your consciousness, rather than the external world. It requires a significant amount of time to navigate these unconventional emotions. If one fails to exercise caution, there is a risk of losing one's sanity. You need to devise a means to regulate those irrational thoughts.

I am aware of your contemplation: How am I expected to accomplish this task? You can do it. If one experiences highly irrational thoughts, it is advisable to seek assistance from a qualified professional. I am referring to a mental health professional, such as a psychiatrist or therapist. An individual capable of providing assistance and offering a confidential space for conversation. I am fortunate to have overcome a significant portion of those intense, distressing thoughts that were sapping my vitality. Those irrational thoughts have not entirely dissipated; they resurface intermittently when my anxiety levels are elevated. I must consistently bear in mind that they are not genuine.

I firmly believe that having a trusted individual with whom one can confide greatly facilitates the process. Furthermore, it would be advantageous if they have experienced or are presently encountering a similar situation. I possess a companion with whom I can readily establish contact at any given time, regardless of the hour. She had been experiencing episodes of anxiety and panic attacks for a period of fifteen years. Fortunately, she possessed the ability to pacify my state of distress. In fact, it was she who informed me of the deep breathing technique. It really does help. I will provide you with the information in a timely manner. In the event that you happen to lack assistance. I highly recommend that you familiarize yourself with this technique. I also suggest that you consider consulting your primary healthcare provider regarding the possibility of receiving medication to assist you in navigating this challenging period. I would recommend seeking an expert who possesses ample patience and expertise in the matter. No, there is a variation among doctors. Undoubtedly, you are already aware of this fact. I would consider taking medication that is guaranteed to be non-addictive. There are a few that are accessible.

Allow me to present an additional idea and resource that I have found to be of great utility. There is no obligation for you to endure these panic attacks. To "ride it out" entails the act of allowing it to run its course. One may posit, similar to enduring a common cold or some such ailment. I am here to apprise you of an alternative approach to cease this occurrence. Prior to its commencement. I will delve into this topic further in subsequent chapters of this book.

Another distressing and irrational notion is the constant preoccupation with one's mortality. I discovered this due to the presence of various indicators associated with anxiety and panic attacks. Similar to the accelerated palpitations of the heart, the distorted visual perception, and the loss of sensation in the facial, upper and lower limbs, as well as the hands and feet. Severe headaches, gastrointestinal discomfort, occasional chest discomfort, and a sensation of throat constriction. Several of these symptoms bear resemblance to those of a heart attack or stroke. While I do not advocate disregarding them initially, it is advisable to do so after several hospital visits and numerous medical consultations and examinations. You have ultimately discerned that it is merely your anxiety manifesting into the onset of a panic attack. It is imperative to engage in mental and physical training in order to cultivate a mindset that recognizes anxiety as a separate entity, thereby avoiding feelings of panic. Engage in internal dialogue, as it proves to be quite beneficial in the current situation. I am confident that you do not desire to make daily visits to the hospital. It is excessively expensive and is likely to exacerbate your condition. Additionally, it depletes one's spirit,

Rest assured that experiencing a panic attack does not pose a risk of mortality or cardiac arrest. It is important to repeatedly affirm this fact to yourself. I am aware that it may seemingly represent one's perception or sentiment. However, it is possible that reminding yourself of this affirmation each time negative emotions arise could potentially prevent the escalation of panic. You are most welcome, ☐.

Remember, self- talk. Tell yourself when the anxiety is ramping up. It appears that your health is stable, as there are no indications of a heart attack or stroke. I am aware that individuals experiencing anxiety often encounter cognitive impairments commonly known as "brain fog." It constitutes an integral aspect of the fluctuating emotions experienced during episodes of anxiety. It is imperative that you cease engaging in self-dialogue and employ breathing techniques as a preventative measure to avert the onset of a panic attack. You can do this. It simply requires dedication and perseverance.

When an undesirable thought infiltrates your mind, simply supplant it with a constructive thought. Convince oneself that these irrational thoughts hold no basis in reality. They will transit within a matter of minutes. Don't be embarrassed. One can engage in self-dialogue in any location, including in public settings. You are also capable of engaging in the deep breathing exercises. They will provide significant assistance.

Additionally, it has come to my attention that the palpitations in my chest are a direct result of the heightened levels of adrenaline coursing through my system. Surprisingly, that proved to be immensely beneficial in alleviating my anxiety. It is imperative that you come to terms with the current circumstances unfolding in your life. Embrace and adapt to your anxiety in order to find contentment in its presence. Acquire the necessary skills to effectively cope with your panic attacks, and over time they may diminish in intensity, and potentially cease altogether. Maintain composure and foster optimistic thoughts to successfully navigate challenging circumstances. I am aware that it may pose initial challenges, yet with the passage of time, one can acquire the ability to rediscover the joys of living. Most of all. Do not concern yourself with the opinions of others. It is within your domain, your struggle. You will win!

Genetics And Heredity

Shyness is often identified as an impediment that hinders individuals in their personal growth and advancement. The inquiry into the cause of shyness has often been raised, however, it has been found that there is a distinct correlation between fear and shyness, indicating that children with higher levels of fear are considerably more inclined to be shy compared to those with lower levels of fear. Shyness can also be observed at a physiological level due to an excess of cortisol. When cortisol is present in higher quantities, it is recognized for its ability to inhibit an individual's immune system, rendering them more susceptible to illness and malady. The study of genetic aspects of shyness is an area of research that has received limited attention, despite the existence of scholarly papers on the biological underpinnings of shyness as far back as 1988. Several studies have indicated a correlation between shyness and aggression, which can be attributed to variants in the DRD4 gene. However, further extensive research is necessary to obtain a comprehensive understanding of this relationship. Moreover, there has been a suggestion that there is an association between shyness and social phobia, although the boundary between the two has become increasingly blurred, with regards to obsessive-compulsive disorder. Likewise, akin to various inquiries into behavioral genetics, the examination of shyness is intricately linked to the number of genes implicated in, and the ambiguity surrounding the characterization of, the phenotype. The act of assigning labels to phenotypes, and the subsequent interpretation of terminology within the fields of genetics and psychology, similarly gives rise to disturbances.

Fear

Fear is an emotional response triggered by perceived threats or hazards, leading to physiological and subsequently societal alterations such as fleeing, concealing, or becoming paralyzed in response to perceived devastating events. Fear in individuals may arise due to a specific stimulus occurring in the present, or as a result of anticipation or apprehension regarding a future threat perceived as a personal risk. The fear response arises from the perception of danger, which leads to engaging in either confrontation or evasion of the threat (also known as the fight-or-flight response), and in extreme cases of fear (such as horror and terror), it can result in a state of immobilization or paralysis.

In both humans and animals, fear is influenced by the process of cognition and acquisition of knowledge. In this manner, fear can be deemed as either rational or appropriate, or as unwarranted or inappropriate. A phobia is the term used to refer to an irrational fear.

Fear is strongly correlated with the sentiment of anxiety, arising from perceiving hazards that are perceived as unpredictable or inevitable. The fear response promotes survival by eliciting appropriate behavioral reactions, and as such, it has been preserved throughout the course of evolution. Sociological and organizational research also suggests that individuals' apprehensions are not solely determined by their predispositions, but are also shaped by their social interactions and cultural environment, which influence their perception of when and to what extent fear should be experienced.

An array of physiological alterations in the body is associated with fear, commonly referred to as the fight-or-flight response. An innate response to adapt to risk, it functions by accelerating the respiratory rate (hyperventilation), heart rate, constriction of the peripheral blood vessels resulting in facial flushing, and intensifying muscle tension, including the muscles attached to each hair follicle causing piloerection or "goosebumps," or more formally known as the clinical term piloerection (which keeps a cold person warmer or makes a startled animal appear more threatening). Additionally, it leads to perspiration, elevated blood glucose levels (hyperglycemia), increased serum calcium levels, an increase in neutrophilic leukocytes (a type of white blood cell), heightened alertness leading to sleep disturbances, and the sensation of "butterflies in the stomach" (dyspepsia). This rudimentary mechanism potentially allows a life form to either retreat or confront the peril it encounters. Through the orchestration of physiological responses, the cognition becomes cognizant of a sensation characterized by trepidation.

The inclination to experience fear is an inherent aspect of human instinct. Extensive research has revealed that certain phobias, such as those related to animals and heights, are notably more prevalent compared to others like floral arrangements or atmospheric phenomena. Additionally, these specific phobias are also more readily induced in controlled laboratory settings according to multiple scientific investigations. This phenomenon is commonly referred to as readiness. Given that individuals who swiftly responded to dangerous situations in ancient times were more likely to survive and reproduce, it is conjectured that the trait of being prepared is a genetically inherited characteristic resulting from natural selection.

From the perspective of evolutionary psychology, a range of fear responses can be regarded as adaptive mechanisms that have proven beneficial in our ancestral heritage. They could have been established over different temporal intervals. Several emotions such as apprehension, such as acrophobia, could be regarded as fundamental across all mammalian species, originating in the Mesozoic era. Varied emotional responses related to fear, such as apprehension towards snakes, could be deemed as typical among all simians and have emerged throughout the Cenozoic era. Furthermore, there are individuals who possess unique phobias such as rodents and insects, which likely originated during the periods of paleolithic and Neolithic eras. This was a time when mice and bugs emerged as significant carriers of diseases and detrimental to crops and stored food supplies.

Learned Fear

Both animals and humans enhance their explicit fear responses through the process of learning. This phenomenon has been extensively examined within the field of psychology, specifically in relation to fear conditioning, with initial research conducted by John B. Watson's investigation on 'Little Albert' conducted in 1920 was inspired by the observation of a child exhibiting an irrationally apprehensive reaction towards canines. Subsequently, the 11-month-old infant was conditioned to develop apprehension towards a white rodent within the confines of the research establishment. The fear gradually encompassed various white, textured objects such as a rabbit, dog, and even a bundle of cotton.

The acquisition of fear can be facilitated through the experience of or observation of a distressing and highly unfortunate incident. As an example, in the event that a child unexpectedly tumbles into a well and exerts effort to escape, it is possible that the person might subsequently develop apprehension towards wells, elevated places (acrophobia), confined spaces (claustrophobia), or bodies of water (aquaphobia). Studies are being conducted to examine brain regions that are susceptible to fear-induced influence. Upon examining these regions, such as the amygdala, it is advised that one must ascertain the capacity to experience fear, be it through personal encounters of trauma or through observing fear in others. In a completed investigation conducted by Andreas Olsson and Katherine I. Nearing and Elizabeth A. Phelps, the amygdala exhibited activity when subjects observed the subjection of another individual to an adverse event, while simultaneously recognizing the anticipation of a similar treatment for themselves. Furthermore, the amygdala also manifested response when subjects were subsequently exposed to a situation that induced fear. This implies that fear can manifest in both situations, not limited solely to personal experiences.

The perception of fear is shaped by the cultural and historical context. To provide an illustration, during the mid-twentieth century, a significant number of individuals in the United States harbored apprehensions regarding polio, which was known to be a potentially fatal affliction. There exists a multitude of distinct approaches that individuals can adopt in response to fear. Display regulations impact the likelihood of individuals exhibiting outward displays of fear and various emotions. Sexual identity may exert an additional influence on feelings of fear. Studies have revealed that individuals of both genders exhibited a stronger inclination to perceive the outward manifestation of fear as more prominent on the countenance of males rather than females. Women also consistently demonstrated superior perception of fear when compared to men.

Apprehension regarding the potential for exploitation is a component of perceived risk and gravity.

Day 13

Exercise:

Attentively listen to an individual without interjecting. Refrain from speaking unless explicitly prompted, and avoid providing extended responses. Shift the conversation focus entirely towards them. Grant them the opportunity to speak and attentively heed their every utterance. Again, do not interrupt. Carefully discern their words and facial expressions without making any presumptions. Maintain composure and equanimity, even in the event of prolonged discourse on their part.

The virtue of patience is waning amidst the advancements of our digital era. It seems evident that all commercial activities are centered around the perceived necessity of achieving increased speed, continuously and repeatedly. Improved response times, expedited uploads, enhanced data capacity, rapid analysis capabilities, accelerated transportation, and a wide range of efficient outcomes. This erroneous desire for velocity has permeated extensively within our shared consciousness. The Western hemisphere is populated with individuals characterized by their high levels of ambition and a sense of urgency, often resulting in a lack of significant progress.

This prevalent absence of patience has given rise to an issue pertaining to reciprocal attentiveness. Additionally, it has led to a significant proliferation of the detrimental attachment to anxiety. Individuals with chronic anxiety possess the anticipation that interpersonal communication will occur at an exceedingly rapid pace. Exercising the virtue of patience through deliberate and attentive listening to an individual's words can effectively decelerate mental activity and foster authentic connections.

It is of utmost importance to deliberately take the time to pause and attentively listen to every individual who engages in conversation with you in the current moment. Patience triumphs over anxiety.

Ten minutes dedicated to ensuring silence and engaging in attentive inhalation and exhalation. Repeat the mantra: "Listen. Be patient. Listen."

(Please consider sharing this experience by using the hashtag #30DAYSPATIENCE)

Day 14

Exercise:

Please take a moment to transcribe onto a sheet of paper, irrespective of its dimensions, the objectives that you have earnestly endeavored to accomplish -

specifically, those aspirations that you perceive to be capable of bestowing upon you a profound sense of contentment. As an illustration: the acquisition of a fresh employment opportunity, the acquisition of a dwelling situated in an affluent locality, embarking on globetrotting expeditions, launching a business venture, establishing a household, forging new social connections, obtaining an academic degree or professional certification, establishing professional contacts, attaining a financial status of one million dollars, and so on.

Now, proceed to rip the paper into several fragments and dispose of them.

Goals can prove to be highly beneficial and advantageous provided they are not excessively fixated upon. Nevertheless, in contemporary society individuals tend to cultivate a dependence on objectives. Consider all of the instances in which you have expressed sentiments such as, "It is imperative that I acquire that," "I am determined to attain this," "I am willing to go to great lengths to achieve that," and so forth. Frequently, individuals devote a greater amount of their time to being preoccupied with their objectives, rather than actively engaging in the present moment to attain them. Furthermore, the objective itself is transitory, whereas the passage in the current moment is tangible and enduring.

The tendency to believe that failure will result if goals are not achieved is subtly ingrained in dependencies. When you have experienced apprehension in previous instances concerning a particular objective, what was the specific goal that induced your anxiety? What was the particular objective you believed it was necessary for you to accomplish?

Ten minutes dedicated to maintaining silence and engaging in focused breathing exercises. Recite the affirmation: "The attainment of a goal does not dictate my happiness." I'm happy now."

(Please kindly consider sharing your experience using the hashtag #30DAYSGOALS)

How To Be A Social Butterfly

"Facilitating the process of transforming into a sociable individual and establishing connections with acquaintances and allies can be achieved by implementing the following strategies:

1. Addressing Any Individual or Group
By employing the skill of discourse, one can engage in conversation with nearly all individuals one encounters, irrespective of any perceived disparities. There exists a shared bond among all individuals, therefore, remain vigilant in your pursuit of acquaintanceship with those whom you desire to comprehend.

2. Engage in the Social Network
Actively contributing to forging strong connections within a community proves to be an effective means of fostering sociability and extroversion. For example, facilitating introductions between individuals can allow you to establish connections with individuals of

diverse backgrounds and forge new relationships. Attend social events where you can engage in networking activities and establish new connections through your existing acquaintances.

3. Know How to Get Past Awkward Silences

Commence speaking when you find yourself amidst a group of individuals. Avoid becoming the individual who has the ability to invariably create uncomfortable situations. Instead, strive to cultivate a reputation as an individual who garners genuine affection and garners hearty laughter in a positive light. Engaging in an initial interaction that dispels initial discomfort and potentially causes momentary self-consciousness is acceptable, as it enables the establishment of trust and garnering of others' approval.

Additionally, it is prudent to engage in an activity that serves to divert attention from uncomfortable periods of silence. An option to consider during a social gathering is to bring along a board game that can be collectively engaged in, thereby facilitating initial interaction.

4. Assume the Role of Party Host

Attending social gatherings can be an exhilarating experience. However, the real complexity of engaging with unfamiliar individuals will arise when you assume the role of the event host. As a host, you are afforded the finest chance to initiate a conversation, create a pleasant atmosphere, acquaint guests with one another, and sustain the flow of activities. By assuming the role of the party host, you may not fully grasp the multitude of opportunities to encounter and connect with a plethora of novel individuals. Please proceed with entering the scene.

Methods For Cultivating Detachment From One's Own Thoughts And Identity?

The human psyche assesses the current circumstances by drawing upon past experiences, thus resulting in a skewed perception. It is often observed that one's own voice can become a significant impediment. Numerous individuals coexist with an internal oppressor that persistently assaults and chastises them, depleting them of essential life force. It is the originating factor behind immeasurable anguish, discontentment, and illness. Thus, it is essential to recognize that genuine vitality and the transformative power it bestows upon our consciousness can only be experienced once the mind is relinquished and our presence in the present moment becomes absolute. This state of enlightenment cannot be comprehended intellectually, but rather, can only be felt. The ego assumes a significant role in orchestrating events within the depths of the subconscious mind. Rooted in the unconscious, the ego perpetuates a distorted perception of self, impeding one from attaining their true identity."

The cognitive mind engages in thinking due to the emergence of negative thoughts that deviate from our true essence. The ego employs past experiences to construct an inaccurate narrative of our identity, drawing from diverse influences such as societal and genetic factors, as well as other minor mental states. For instance, the consumption of alcohol can impair judgment and affect human conduct.

The capacity for decision-making

Eckhart Tolle elucidates this concept in precise fashion. Pages 188-189 contain the passage pertaining to the word "choose," a term that finds regular utilization in our daily interactions. However, opting for such terminology can be deceptive when asserting that an individual deliberately selects a maladaptive relationship or any other circumstance within their life. The concept of choice necessitates a substantial level of consciousness, as without it, one's ability to exercise choice becomes null and void. The exercise of choice commences as soon as one erroneously perceives the mind and its conditioned patterns, and continues until one attains presence. Prior to this, one remains spiritually unaware and devoid of conscious choice. This implies that you are obligated to contemplate, experience, and behave in a specific manner. In accordance with the state of your mental faculties. At that moment, Jesus uttered the words, "Forgive them, for they are unaware of the consequences of their actions." This is not correlated with intelligence in the conventional interpretation of the term. I have encountered numerous individuals who possess high levels of intelligence and education, yet exhibit a lack of awareness. Given that one's consciousness remains stagnant, meaning that they have become wholly encompassed by their own thoughts, can you comprehend the potential consequences that may arise from such a state?

One does not possess a choice when they are being manipulated by the subconscious mind, signifying a lack of awareness of reality and adherence to preconceived mental frameworks that dictate the perceived needs of the world, thereby resulting in an absence of complete presence in the current moment. This also causes the male companion of the girl to lose consciousness as his mental faculties are also affected.

Given the predisposition of mental and emotional thought patterns, the inquiry arises as to whether one's true essence aligns with these patterns. in her regards no. This is how the mind seeks to establish its sense of identity. If one is unable to tap into the potency of the current moment, which permits one to transcend the influence of an ingrained past, she will be faced with a decision. Therefore, if you possess lingering ill will towards your parents, you are nurturing deeply rooted animosity. The emotional distress arising from this stems from your lack of complete mindfulness. It is also imperative to acknowledge that they, too, were devoid of alternatives. One can only exercise their freedom of choice if they have achieved a state of mind unfettered by constraints.

For instance, a young woman finds herself in an unfavorable relationship, not due to her active choice, but rather because her perception of reality is clouded. This is a result of her unconsciousness regarding the impact of her childhood experiences, which her mind has normalized and come to accept as the standard pattern of thought processes.

Consider reflecting on the previous occasion when an unpleasant dream caused you to experience feelings of anger or sadness upon waking. Examples may include scenarios such as the loss of a loved one or discovering infidelity within a spouse. During this time, the mind generated fictitious images that elicited emotional reactions within us. These outwardly expressed emotions truly reflected the state of our inner mind. However, we must strive to disregard these thoughts and detach ourselves from the workings of the mind. Instead, we should cultivate heightened awareness of the present moment. This process also encompasses the concept of the pain body. The identical factors that regulate our emotions stem from the cognitive patterns we perceive.

However, refrain from attempting to comprehend it through your intellect. Do not endeavor to comprehend it. One can acquire this knowledge solely when the mind achieves a state of calmness. When one is in a state of utmost presence, with undivided and intense focus on the present moment, the essence of existence can be experienced, yet it surpasses the realm of intellectual comprehension.

On page 18, it is asserted that the mind can be regarded as an instrument or a tool. It is intended for utilization in a particular undertaking, and once the undertaking is accomplished, it is relinquished. Given the present circumstances, I would assert that approximately 80 to 90 percent of individuals' cognitive processes are not only repetitive and impulsively unproductive, but also detrimental owing to their dysfunctional and frequently pessimistic disposition. If you take the opportunity to carefully examine your thoughts, you will discover that this statement holds true. It precipitates a consequential dissipation of essential vitality. Is this type of excessive thinking considered an addiction? Quite frankly, you no longer perceive yourself as having the freedom to cease. It appears to possess superior strength compared to you. Moreover, it instills within individuals a deceptive notion of joy, a joy that inevitably transitions into agony.

What is the rationale behind developing a dependency on contemplation? Due to the fact that you are associated with it, consequently deriving your sense of identity from the content and operation of your mind. Due to the conviction you held that ceasing to think would result in the cessation of your existence. As one progresses through life, an individual develops a cognitive representation of their identity, which is shaped by their unique personal experiences and the influence of their cultural environment. We can designate this spectral self as the ego. It encompasses cognitive engagement and can be sustained solely through persistent mental activity. The concept of ego carries varied interpretations based on individual perspectives. However, in the present context, its connotation refers to the misleading representation of oneself, stemming from an unconscious attachment to the workings of the mind.

◆

Rather than entertaining negative possibilities, endeavor to substitute them with positive ones.

The ego continually engages in comparative analysis with others, resulting in feelings of inadequacy or insignificance when perceiving others as possessing more than oneself. However, it is essential to recognize that material possessions do not define an individual's true worth, as they hold no significance in the realm beyond mortal existence.

In due course, we will need to acknowledge the inevitability of transitioning towards an afterlife. To dispel apprehension towards entering this realm, it is imperative that we construct within our minds a vision of the afterlife as an exquisite abode awaiting our arrival.

1) Research indicates that performing this exercise while observing oneself in the mirror with a demeanor of

despondency can provide insight into one's outward posture in such a state. Subsequently, engaging in power poses involving hands placed on the hips or crossed arms has been discovered to elicit feelings of empowerment and notably enhance testosterone levels.

2) If you are an individual who has made certain regrettable errors, it is advisable to refrain from labeling them as mere mistakes, but rather as instances of temporary lapse in judgment that all human beings are prone to experiencing. Such lapses occur when our thought processes momentarily waver, and are unrelated to our inherent nature, but rather attributable to common human tendencies.

Achieving presence: In a heightened state of being,
Engage in this brief activity by gently closing your eyes and envisioning a scenario where you have unfortunately lost your sense of sight, enduring a decade of blindness. However, in a

miraculous turn of events, when you open your eyes once more, a profound transformation occurs, granting you the ability to perceive your surroundings. Consider the emotions and sentiments that would arise in this moment, particularly as you cast your gaze upon a cherished individual in your life - whether it be your son, daughter, mother, or father - witnessing their countenance for the very first time after an extended period of blindness spanning ten years. Channel all of your emotions into directing your attention towards your surroundings, allowing yourself to deeply perceive the atmosphere and the various elements that surround you. Consequently, you will develop a heightened sense of gratitude towards life. This state of heightened awareness can be referred to as enlightenment or complete presence.

Assume Your Individual Responsibilities And Exercise Authority.

When endeavoring to address anxiety disorder, it is common for individuals to promptly seek professional assistance without initially acknowledging the significance of creating a sense of comfort during the transient experience of anxiety. Prior to seeking the guidance of a counselor, it is imperative to remind oneself that this sentiment shall dissipate in due course. Furthermore, it is crucial to focus on fostering a state of holistic comfort, encompassing both physical and emotional well-being. In order to accomplish this, it will be necessary for you to:

Recognize the scenario - when we engage in combat with anxiety, we effectively amplify its strength. Recognizing and acknowledging the presence of anxiety is an initial step towards mitigating its impact. One of the most highly suggested methods to engage in this entails the subsequent course of action:

Allocate approximately 15 minutes to deliberately evoke a significant level of anxiety within yourself. Furthermore, it is imperative that you cultivate a mindset characterized by intense apprehension. Strive to elevate your anxiety levels to their utmost extent. Make an effort to maintain it in that position for at least a duration of five minutes. It is likely that you will encounter difficulty in maintaining a sufficiently elevated level of anxiety. This particular method of exposure technique aids in mitigating anxiety.

Engage in constructive internal dialogue - The majority of our self-talk while experiencing an anxiety disorder tends to exacerbate our feelings of anxiety. It is advisable that you engage in reaffirming statements to yourself, such as:

I shall overcome this" "I am determined to persevere" "I am committed to overcoming this obstacle" "I have the resolve to navigate through this" "I am confident in my ability to overcome this challenge

The sensation will eventually dissipate.

I am currently in a secure state

Despite my current anxiety, I shall attain a state of tranquility.

I am presently experiencing a gradual decrease in my heart rate.

Divert your attention – Occasionally, it can be helpful to divert your attention away from the anxiety you may be experiencing and direct it towards another task or activity. If you are able to effectively divert your attention to a different subject matter, you will experience enhanced ease in managing symptoms of anxiety.

Relaxation techniques - Among the primary means employed by the body in combating anxiety is the practice of relaxation, which essentially acts to counteract the physiological stress response. Initiate the utilization of expeditious relaxation techniques to elicit the relaxation response and alleviate manifestations of anxiety. Several accessible techniques for relaxation include engaging in aromatherapy, immersing oneself in uplifting melodies, practicing deep breathing exercises, and receiving a massage, among other viable options.

Rapid Strategies To Employ When Experiencing Elevated Levels Of Stress

It can be quite astonishing to discover that stress is genuinely transmissible. Recent scientific research has substantiated this fact. In spite of the utilization of animals as the focal point in the research, the outcome carries substantial significance. Consequently, this truth is also applicable to the human species. In the aforementioned study, it was observed by the authors that the stress experienced by one individual can be transmitted or acquired by another.

The ramifications of the study could have a noteworthy impact on each individual within our collective. It might imply that attending to an individual experiencing stress can potentially exert an adverse influence on one's mental and emotional state.

It is probable that exposure to sorrowful narratives can induce feelings of stress. Alternatively, it is possible that your friend has already experienced increased stress as a result of the negative encounter you recounted.

Professor Bains is cognizant of this potential outcome. "We involuntarily transmit our stress to others, often without conscious awareness," Bains supplemented. There is compelling evidence suggesting that certain manifestations of stress can endure within the immediate relations and significant others of individuals grappling with post-traumatic stress disorder (PTSD). In the event that you are already experiencing stress, how might one address and mitigate such circumstances? Would you be able to alleviate the stress?

There might not be a singular response to these inquiries. However, a variety of tactics exist that can mitigate your psychological stress.

1. Cease excessive consumption of caffeine, tobacco, and alcohol.

Refrain from the consumption of caffeinated beverages, nicotine, and alcoholic beverages. These substances are stimulants. Consequently, these substances have the potential to elevate one's stress levels.

An alternative course of action is to consume ample amounts of water, herbal infusions, and fruit-based beverages. Fruits possess inherent nutritional components that serve to enhance both your physical and psychological well-being.

2. Stay active

There are numerous factors that can contribute to feelings of distress. Possible alternatives: - This may pertain to various aspects of your life, such as your occupation, personal relationships, and financial circumstances. - These factors could encompass different dimensions of your life, including your professional commitments, intimate connections, and economic challenges. - This encompasses a range of areas in your life, such as your career, romantic partnerships, and financial situations. - It could relate to diverse facets of your life, including your employment, interpersonal connections, and financial burdens. - This applies to various spheres of your life, comprising your professional occupation, interpersonal associations, and financial predicaments. If you perceive that you have reached a state of mental or physical exhaustion, it is advisable to cease your current activities. I suggest embarking on a leisurely stroll to inhale the invigorating outdoor atmosphere. If it is possible, it would be advisable to visit the gym. Engaging in physical exercises can be beneficial for promoting relaxation of both the body and mind. By engaging in the act of mental relaxation, you not only bolster your psychological well-being but also facilitate the overall restoration of your physicality.

Each instance in which an individual perceives a threat, their physiological system initiates a response. The brain transmits a signal to the adrenal gland prompting the secretion of a hormone known as adrenaline.

The adrenal gland is classified as an endocrine gland, implying that the biochemical substances it secretes will be dispersed throughout the bloodstream. Subsequently, the adrenaline that is released will enter the bloodstream, consequently leading to elevated blood sugar levels, augmented heart rate, and increased blood pressure. Subsequently, the hypothalamus, a region within the brain, will transmit a signal to the pituitary gland. This gland will secrete substances that will elicit the activation of the adrenal cortex, leading to the secretion of cortisol. Cortisol functions as a hormone that is released in response to stressful situations. It facilitates the body in producing sufficient energy to enable escape from the perilous circumstances. Nevertheless, the excessive presence of cortisol within the bloodstream will have detrimental effects on the functionality of the immune system. Moreover, it has the capacity to cause harm to the neuronal structures of the brain, thereby potentially leading to cognitive dysfunction manifested as memory deficits. Indeed, it is worth noting that in numerous instances, chronic stress may additionally precipitate the occurrence of stroke and myocardial infarction.

The strain and cognitive load

Research conducted over the past few decades has indicated that there is a potential detrimental impact of stress on the brain. An excessive quantity of cortisol can cause cellular damage in the hippocampus region, compromising its role in the retention of memories. Furthermore, numerous research studies have indicated that chronic stress can lead to the premature aging of brain cells.

The stress hormone cortisol plays a crucial role in the maintenance of your survival. However, excessive consumption of it is certainly detrimental. Persistent stress can also lead to depressive symptoms and other psychological disorders.

How can one safeguard their mind against the impacts of stress?

Alleviating stress frequently necessitates the use of medication. However, a recent study has uncovered an uncomplicated approach to alleviate stress without incurring any expenses. The study revealed that engaging in regular running can have a significantly positive impact on alleviating stress. Indeed, the study posits that engaging in running activities has the capability to effectively counteract the impact of stress on neuronal cells within the brain.

Dr. Jeff Edwards, the renowned academician, expounded upon the findings. According to Edwards, engaging in physical activity is a straightforward and economical method to mitigate the adverse effects of persistent stress on one's memory. Optimal learning outcomes can be achieved when individuals remain devoid of stress. The implications of this finding are significant for both scholarly and practical contexts.

In order to effectively cope with stress and maintain optimal cognitive function, it is imperative to allocate a portion of your schedule for engaging in a modest form of physical exertion, such as engaging in a running routine. This exercise represents a straightforward method to cultivate psychological and mental well-being.

"It is indeed empowering to realize that mitigating the adverse effects of stress on our cognitive faculties is achievable through the simple act of engaging in jogging or running," Edwards further articulated.

Reading The Eyes

The eyes are frequently referred to as the portals to one's inner self with good reason, as they possess remarkable powers of expression. When you cast a brief gaze upon another individual's eyes, you engage in several crucial actions. First, it is essential to recognize their presence and existence. This is of utmost significance—when you engage in this behavior, you demonstrate a sincere and attentive focus on their concerns. By actively demonstrating your attentive presence, you convey your commitment to offering them your undivided attention. The ability to direct one's attention to the eyes typically affords inherent advantages, as one dedicates the necessary time to interpret visual cues such as gaze patterns, pupil dilation, and the frequency of eye contact.

Reading Gaze

The observation of one's gaze can provide significant insights into the individual being observed. More specifically, there are two fundamental factors that should be taken into account when endeavoring to interpret the visual focus of another individual. One must take into consideration both the location and the duration. Nevertheless, acquiring the knowledge to effectively interpret this particular aspect of the human anatomy enables one to gain profound insights into the cognitive processes occurring within another individual's psyche.

The direction of one's gaze plays a significant role, as it may suggest the person's desire if they focus their attention on an object. Observing the individual directing their attention towards the door and simultaneously fixating on a piece of cake may suggest that the cake is the current subject of their longing or desire. By acquiring the skill of accurately discerning the direction of another individual's gaze, one can typically deduce the object of their interest and subsequently determine the nature of the attention -

whether positive or negative - by observing the remaining cues displayed through body language.

- Gaze duration: The period of time allocated to fixating on an object also conveys significant insights. By observing the duration of another individual's focused gaze, one can discern the necessary steps to comprehend their actions and thoughts. You desire to ascertain your understanding that their actions are entirely influenced by the object of their focus. In general, the greater the duration of someone's intense gaze, the higher value they ascribe to or the more captivating they perceive the object of their attention to be.

Reading eye contact

When desiring to establish eye contact with another individual, it is crucial to bear in mind that eye contact, as a general rule, tends to carry a significant level of intensity. This can quickly be perceived as incorrect or excessively assertive if one lacks proficiency in the matter. Nonetheless, insufficient levels of direct gaze are also considered concerning as they suggest a lack of genuine interest or potential deceit. The appropriate level of eye contact entails maintaining visual contact for approximately 70% of the time. Please be advised that excessive staring may be interpreted as aggressive behavior, resulting in an outcome contrary to your intended objective.

Analyzing the expansion of the pupils

Pupillary dilation ensues when the irises of the eyes undergo expansion. Conversely, unless in close proximity or encountering individuals with darker eye colors that effectively obscure their pupils, it can be challenging to detect such indications. Nevertheless, upon closer observation of closed eyes, it is possible to discern the dilation of the pupils. The aspect pertaining to pupil dilation lies in its inherent inability to be manipulated—conscious control over the dilation of one's pupils is unattainable. Consequently, it emerges as a reasonably dependable indicator.

Generally, the expansion of the pupils is observed when an individual directs their gaze towards a person or object that elicits desire or attraction. When one encounters a stimulus that exerts a greater allure, the typical response observed is the expansion of the pupil. However, it should be noted that the pupils will also undergo dilation in response to cognitive processing. In the case of engaging in intricate mathematical calculations, such as those of a complex nature, a notable physiological response can be observed, namely the dilation of the pupils.

Reading the Eyebrows
The individuals to whom the eyebrows belong have much to convey. They serve to outline the eyes and facilitate an enhanced level of expressiveness. When you take a look at the eyebrows, you see that arch over the eyes that are free to move in most directions. Specifically, you will discover that observing the eyebrows yields significant information. Please observe the following signs.

Raised

Elevating the eyebrows often conveys a desire to assimilate one's environment to a greater extent. You may be nurturing their capacity for perception or enhancing the emphasis on a certain aspect that you also wish to inquire about. For instance, it has the potential to necessitate the expression of an inquiry or to manifest uncertainty regarding a given circumstance.

Raising inner corners

By elevating the medial ends of your eyebrows, particularly as you converge them in the middle, you express either unease or solace. You will need to consider alternative indicators to ascertain which option is better suited for this particular situation.

Lowered

When one intentionally depresses their eyebrows, it creates the effect of partially veiling or concealing their eyes, as if deliberately obscuring them from sight. Additionally, you are demonstrating a heightened level of concentration by directing your gaze specifically towards a single entity, indicating a strong level of attentiveness towards the object of your fixation. This behavior is commonly indicative of feelings of annoyance or asserting dominance, although it can also serve as an expression of anger, depending on the presence of other facial cues.

Lowering center

When examining the midpoint of the brows, it is possible for them to converge, forming a V-shaped pattern. Upon the occurrence of this phenomenon, minute creases materialize in that area, thereby originating the distinctive form. Typically, this indicates a state of intense focus or possible exasperation.

Engaging in repetitive lowering and raising.

When the eyebrows are raised and lowered in a repetitive manner, particularly at a rapid pace, one is engaging in the action of wiggling them. This typically stems from a desire to attract someone's attention or alternatively, to acknowledge their presence. It can also be utilized to demonstrate an intensified state of astonishment.

Reading the Cheeks

The buccal region constitutes the majority of one's facial structure, and yet it is frequently overlooked in the context of interpreting nonverbal cues. Nonetheless, it is imperative to give considerable attention to these aspects, and it is essential to diligently concentrate on them to the utmost of your capabilities. In essence, by considering other body parts simultaneously, examining the cheeks will ultimately aid in determining one's actions. By acquiring the skill of interpreting facial expressions, you will gain an additional insight into the mental state of the individual.

Cheeks pulled in

When an individual's cheeks are retracted, it is generally indicative of their vexation, particularly when accompanied by the pursing of the lips.

Moreover, it is imperative to take this into careful consideration. It is generally advisable to refrain from inconveniencing an individual exhibiting such behavior.

Cheeks blown out

If one observes the bulging of their cheeks, one observes their act of expanding them. They appear inflated, a tendency that often arises due to exaggerated reactions as a manifestation of uncertainty or a sense of being somewhat overwhelmed by the multitude of tasks that need to be accomplished. When you contemplate this course of action, it is typically indicative of significant disapproval.

Cheeks turning red

When facial coloration shifts toward a rosy hue, it commonly arises from feelings of distress or ire elicited by a particular circumstance. Seek additional indicators that can assist in elucidating their thoughts.

Cheeks paling

On the contrary, when one's cheeks shift towards a paler complexion, it becomes evident that a sudden depletion of blood has occurred in their facial region. This typically indicates that the blood flow has been redirected to alternative areas, such as the lower extremities for locomotion. It frequently indicates a condition of apprehension or doubt. Nevertheless, it could also indicate that the ambient temperature is low.

Masticating the interior surface of the buccal cavity

When one engages in the act of biting the inside of their cheek, it can be inferred that apprehension or anxiety is being experienced in relation to the present circumstances. Your display of tentative assurance and inclination to self-comfort indicate a degree of uncertainty concerning the progress of affairs. Furthermore, it may also indicate a deliberate effort to refrain from uttering phrases that are likely to evoke difficulties, such as those that would perpetuate the falsehoods you are disseminating.

Caressing the facial region

Through the act of placing your hand on your cheek, you are effectively conveying a sense of hyperbole or intensified emphasis regarding the occurrence at hand. Typically, the placement of both hands upon both cheeks denotes the expression of heightened emotion, such as astonishment or dismay.

Anxiousness As A Response To Ambiguity

In the initial segment of this book, I posited the notion that anxiety, despite its discomfort, serves as a pivotal indicator. It provides insight into the presence of potential risks and serves as a driving force for our proactive efforts to prepare and mitigate said risks. Due to the pervasive existence of potential risks, it is customary to encounter a sense of anxiety on a recurrent basis. Such a feeling of anxiety is expected and advantageous.

Anxiety is inherent in the human condition, as it arises from the ever-present presence of uncertainty and the possibility of risks. We hold the belief that experiencing anxiety in such circumstances should not be classified as a disorder. Nevertheless, on certain occasions, the circumstances could be exceedingly extraordinary, surpassing the realm of typical human encounters. Therefore, the excessive levels of anxiety that an individual may encounter could potentially fall beyond the average range and meet the criteria for a recognized psychological condition. The anxiety observed is commonly identified as reactive anxiety due to its justifiable occurrence in response to the extraordinary circumstances faced by the individual. However, it reaches such an exacerbated level that it impairs their ability to effectively carry out daily activities.

Anxiety as an Indirect Consequence of a Pathological Progression

Our physical forms are awe-inspiring mechanisms that embody a intricate equilibrium. In our physiological systems, there exists a complex web of interconnectedness where each component interacts harmoniously with one another. If our body becomes overheated due to prolonged sun exposure on a scorching day, it is not merely a sensation of being hot that we encounter. Numerous other physiological processes will be impacted, with certain functions extending beyond our conscious perception. These reactions are severe in nature and have the potential to pose a risk to an individual's life. That assertion holds true for illnesses of any nature. A pathological condition, such as cancer, may display its effects predominantly on a specific organ, consequently manifesting primary symptoms resulting from the organ's malfunction. Nevertheless, it is highly likely that the malignancy will exert an influence on adjacent organs as a result of their interconnectedness with the cancer-stricken organ.

The components of the brain that elicit anxiety are organs that encounter the influence of numerous other systems within our physiological framework. It is often observed that diseases can directly induce a sense of anxiety by interfering with normal bodily functioning. Kindly observe the precise phrasing employed in the preceding statement. The sensation of unease arises from the stimulation of specific brain regions involved in anxiety, which occurs indirectly as a result of the progression of the disease. Nevertheless, it is inconsequential whether said sentiment arises from an indirect stimulus due to a medical condition or a direct stimulus stemming from the circumstances in which we are situated. In both instances, we will experience apprehension, and in both scenarios, we will react to such unease.

There is another way in which a disease process can create anxiety as a secondary effect. Indeed, numerous individuals would contend that this mechanism does not constitute a derivative outcome. When one receives a diagnosis of cancer or any other potentially fatal illness, it becomes challenging to refrain from experiencing heightened apprehension regarding such circumstances. There may be limited alternatives available to you besides pursuing effective medical care and actively participating in the treatment protocol. However, being in a circumstance where there is a potential risk of mortality can undeniably evoke feelings of anxiety.

Certain individuals attempt to manage this anxiety by upholding an impractical optimistic perspective. Psychologists would categorize this reaction as denial, however, it is not obligatory to consistently adopt a realistic perspective on the world. I strongly advise against denial; rather, I suggest that you acknowledge the importance of addressing the anxiety. There are various therapeutic interventions available to alleviate anxiety, specifically in cases where individuals confront their own mortality. Additionally, there is substantiated evidence indicating that the management of such anxiety significantly enhances the likelihood of a positive prognosis for recuperation (Yusufov et al., 2020). Therefore, in the event that an individual or their dear one is afflicted with a life-threatening ailment, it is advisable to pursue superior medical intervention as well as complementary psychological support. During this critical period, not only will the patient experience heightened levels of comfort, but there will also be an enhanced probability of survival from the illness.

Vitamins

It is of paramount importance to maintain a daily regimen of vitamin intake. This will aid in the alleviation of your anxiety by inducing a state of relaxation in your nervous system. Experiencing anxiety can often diminish one's appetite, thereby emphasizing the importance of ensuring adequate nutritional intake through regular consumption of essential vitamins. Insufficient nutrients are depleted from the body when it is under stress. The acquisition of adequate nutrients shall bestow your body with vitality.

Vitamin K
Kale is a highly nutritious vegetable that is abundant in vitamin K. Consuming an adequate amount of green vegetables will contribute to maintaining a high

level of energy throughout the duration of the day. Facilitating optimal bodily functioning to mitigate feelings of fatigue. Consuming an adequate quantity of green-leafy vegetables can contribute to the alleviation of anxiety. Vitamin K can also be obtained in the form of capsules from retail establishments.

Vitamin B
Ensure that you acquire your daily dose of vitamin B, as this particular nutrient has been recognized for its beneficial effects on anxiety, emotional equilibrium, and agitation. Consistently incorporating a daily regimen of vitamin B intake has been shown to effectively alleviate anxiety symptoms, while also contributing to the body's holistic nutritional requirements on a daily basis. Prominent dietary sources of vitamin B encompass turkey, bananas, whole grains, and potatoes.

Vitamin D

This vitamin is of utmost significance and should be consumed regularly. One could obtain a sufficient quantity of vitamin D by basking in the sun or alternatively, one may acquire this vitamin through an over-the-counter purchase and ingest it in capsule form. The consumption of Vitamin D has been found to have a calming effect on anxiety, therefore it would be prudent to increase outdoor activities to facilitate adequate synthesis of this essential nutrient within the body. Whether you engage in physical activity, such as taking a walk to enhance your well-being – which incidentally aids in alleviating anxiety – it is advisable to occasionally expose yourself to sunlight, as your body necessitates this vital nutrient.

Vitamin C
This vitamin has proven efficacy in modulating brain chemistry, thereby aiding in the reduction of anxiety levels. It is recommended to incorporate a daily

regimen of a substantial amount of vitamin C to effectively alleviate feelings of anxiety. Consuming vitamin C daily is highly recommended to bolster the immune system, thereby reducing the susceptibility to illnesses and mitigating potential complications stemming from anxiety-related effects on one's overall well-being.

Vitamin E
This vitamin helps transport oxygen to the brain hence reducing your anxiety. Incorporating vitamin E into your daily vitamin regimen would be beneficial for optimizing cognitive function, as well as mitigating stress levels. Vitamin E can be found abundantly in corn, soybeans, peanuts, hazelnuts, and almonds.

Indications of Inadequate Attachment
Insecurity gives rise to certain practices that stem from attachments. Early adolescence can give rise to a variety of

unfavorable patterns that manifest due to unreliable connections.

Too Demanding

As an example, it is undesirable for one's partner to accomplish tasks independently and exclude oneself from the process. Your intention is to allocate a significant portion of both your and their leisure time towards shared activities. You command their undivided attention and due regard, often to the detriment of their other affiliations and connections.

Doubt or Jealousy

As an illustration, if you harbor doubts regarding the behavior of your partner or associate and the individuals they associate with. You inquire about their professional affiliations and the individuals they engage with within their professional sphere.

You exhibit a sense of apprehension towards individuals whom you perceive as developing close relationships with, as you harbor a fear of abandonment and potential infidelity.

Lack of Emotional Intimacy

For example, your associate or significant other genuinely expresses an inability to establish close proximity with you. They depict you as an individual who "establishes boundaries" or assert that you are frequently challenging to emotionally approach.

Enthusiastic Dependency

You depend on your companion or partner for your emotional well-being. You seek for your happiness to stem from your interpersonal connections. If one is experiencing distress, it implies a perception of insufficient satisfaction from one's partner or companion.

Frightful

You seek intimacy and depth in your relationships. Notwithstanding, it has been your observation that when you come into close proximity with your significant other, they inflict harm upon you. This leads to a mixture of emotions being experienced by you.

You initiate proximity with your partner, only to subsequently withdraw when it reaches a threshold considered overwhelming. Fearing potential emotional injury, your apprehension towards becoming intimately involved detrimentally impacts the quality of your relationship.

Absence of Trust

You refrain from divulging your thoughts and emotions to your companion due to apprehension that they might undermine your trust or abandon you. You harbor apprehension that divulging certain aspects about yourself may not be well-received by them, potentially leading to the termination of the relationship.

www.ingramcontent.com/pod-product-compliance
Lightning Source LLC
Chambersburg PA
CBHW050256120526
44590CB00016B/2371